STILL

TONY HARRIS

Copyright © 2017 Tony Harris
All rights reserved

ISBN-13: 9781548305659
ISBN-10: 1548305650

Still

Tony Harris, Author

Copyright © 2017 Tony Harris
Pam Ryans, Publishing Liaison
www.pamryans.com

All Rights Reserved.

No parts of this book may be reproduced or transmitted in any manner whatsoever, or stored in any information storage system, without the prior written consent/permission from the publisher or the author except in the case of brief quotations with proper reference, embodied in critical articles and reviews.

ISBN-13: 9781548305659
ISBN-10: 1548305650

Printed and Manufactured in the United States of America

TONY HARRIS

DEDICATION

STILL is dedicated to my grandmother Viola Savage who's interdependence on Christ has shaped and made me who I am. What a blessed woman!

CONTENTS

	Acknowledgments	i
1	Tomorrow Never Comes	3
2	Still	4
3	A Flower Grows	6
4	Yes, I Am Ready	8
5	Refreshed	10
6	Carry Me Away	12
7	The Feast	14
8	Unto Thee	18
9	Until Death Do Us Part	20
10	In You	24
11	There Is A Continuation	27
12	I Am Blessed	28
13	With God's Own Love	30
14	Come	32
15	Draw Me	34
16	Who Can Question	36
17	As A Child	38
18	Bring Out	40
19	He Talks To Me	42

20	I Am Learning	44
21	On the Wings of Love	46
22	Because Of You	48
23	Marching On	50
24	Only For A Moment	51
25	The Fire Burns	53
25	For You	55
26	All Things are New	56
27	Life Goes On	58
28	Keep Me	60
29	Through Your Eyes	61
30	Reflecting	63
31	I Took One Step	65
32	A Taste of Heaven	67
33	Dreams	69
34	I Have Lived My Dream	60
35	This Is Mine	72
36	Calling On Jesus	74
37	You Fixed it for Me	76
38	Outside the Storm is Raging	78
39	Hinder Me, But Don't Stop Me	80
40	It Doesn't Really Matter	81

41	I Am A Child of God	83
42	The Way	85
43	When Times Draw Nigh	87
44	The Curtains of Memories	89
45	Blame Not	92
46	People Do Not Know	94
47	Talent	96
48	Whatever	98
49	Facets	99
50	I Can Say	100
51	Teach Me Humbleness	101
52	I Shall	102
53	Watch Out	104
54	With My	106
55	There Shall be Rest	108
56	The Smile?	109
57	Even Though	110
58	With the Quickness	112
59	Consume	113
60	Sunrise to Glory	115
61	He IS	117
62	I'm Gonna Live	119

63	The Rainbow	121
64	My Telephone Lover	122
63	We	124
64	To John Keats	126
	About the Author	128

ACKNOWLEDGMENTS

Thank you God for revealing yourself to me and allowing me to depend on you for everything. Because, without you I have nothing. Thank you for the life lessons you teach me. Lord you have put so many in my life that have prayed and encouraged me to continue to seek you in my living and giving. Most importantly, I want to thank Pam Ryans for all the grooming and encouragement, I need to be continually effective to do your will. Amen.

Tomorrow Never Comes

Today is here, never to be seen again.

I have lived this day, today

All my dreams have been accomplished.

When I see this day tomorrow,

It becomes yesterday.

TONY HARRIS

Still

After so many years of waiting, searching and hoping,

Looking but never finding,

Listening but never hearing,

And touching but never feeling.

After so many lonely hours of trying to find myself,

Analyzing inside and out,

Backwards, forwards, upwards and down,

Still I found nothing, no reason to be proud.

For I had once touched the risen Lord.

Once I looked, I found many answers.

I reached out, and felt his tender touch.

I even heard the still small voice,

So sweetly in my ears.

And still I went my merry way,

Doing the things that felt, oh God so right.

But there you stood, so patiently waiting,

STILL

Beckoning me to come and try again.

To open my eyes, for a new day has dawned,

The sun shines so bright.

Still, you stand there with arms opened wide.

You even showed me mercy, after crucifying you afresh.

And though I thought myself lost, even without hope.

Again, you came to abide within.

Showing me that you are forever and still.

A Flower Grows

Lord, take the seed and plant it in the rich moist soil,

That my roots may be healthy and strong.

Water me dutifully and daily,

So I can grow just right.

Out of the ground, I shall spring forth!

With the first green leaf to show my appreciation,

For the tender loving kindness shown.

Don't stop working and tilling the soil,

Because I'm still growing and I need continual pruning.

As the days pass, I will stand tall and straight.

My stem glistens in gratitude for the nourishments.

The buds are forming and reaching towards the sky.

Then you will look and see how hard I try.

To bloom open my face with the crisp early morning dew,

Reflecting all the tedious work of the gardener's hand.

STILL

Beaming forth in luster of all the care given.

Elegantly growing into the beauty I was meant to be.

When I have grown into my fullness,

Let all the world pass by your window,

Just to see how beautiful a flower grows.

Yes, I Am Ready

Yes, I am ready to turn my back on the world,

For all within, shall soon pass away.

Nothing has the world to offer me.

Its darkness abounds the boarders of my security.

Yes, I am ready to give up its blood guilty thirst,

To wash away that deadly poison from my being.

Ah! Smell the sweetness.

Yes, I am ready to learn of an undying love.

That guarantees just as promised,

And delivers perfection abound.

All in the world has died, nothing has survived.

Yes, I am ready for a closer walk with thee.

Where I can be confident and trusting with childlike faith.

To be able to follow you to the ends of the world,

Knowing I have the protection of your abiding love.

STILL

Yes Lord, I am ready to be sheltered from the storm.

Tuck me safely away from the ferociousness,

Inside, I will be toasty and warm.

Knowing that my safety is assured.

Ask of me and I shall pray my strength in the Lord.

Delegate my duties, and I will desperately try to perform,

To bring all my obligations into conformity.

And yes, you shall see, I am ready to do thy biding.

Refreshed!

He touched me again and again!

Brought me happiness, from deep within

The peace I feel just cannot be compared.

There is no one anywhere,

Who can show me greater care?

For I have been refreshed by the power of God.

Refreshed in my drive and determination to go forth.

Never shall I look behind to see the long and winding road.

Nor, shall I stand awaiting in the wings to take my stand.

Because Jesus has the power I shall always need.

Refreshed!

Refreshed!

Refreshed is the feeling I feel today!

Because I can call upon the Lord,

For all his dependability.

I know he will hear my plea.

STILL

He loved me even though I knew him not.

He forgave my transgressions, and returned my soul to me.

Gave me all the love I needed,

So I could be refreshed!

Carry Me Away

Carry me away from a land so sick.

Starvation has left many to die.

A place where hate thrives at every corner turned.

A land where there is no peace, nor can it be found.

Carry me away from this world of woes and sorrows.

Where a child has only traits of hopelessness and hate.

Where the destruction of others advances the gain.

A world that has no love, or joy,

To brighten the darkest day.

Take me to a place where thankfulness dwells all day.

Where joy to my soul fills my every need.

A place to forget all my troubles and woes.

That I maybe able to love in all truth and sincerity.

Take me there Lord, would you, will you please?

So I may grow in strength and grace.

STILL

Take me to a land where the Lord's face

Shines instead of the sun.

Where there is happiness, peace and joy to fill everyone.

Carry me away on your wings of mercy,

Hold me tight with the grips of righteousness.

That I may withstand the fiery furnace,

To live an everlasting life,

In the presence of Christ.

The Feast

Dinner time and the table is full.

Full of all the wonderful decorative dishes,

In which a soul can feast.

Love.

For there is no greater love,

Than to sacrifice the life of a son.

Charity.

Humbleness in spirit,

For all things given.

Hope.

Where there is hope,

There is the Christ.

Faith.

For without faith nothing is impossible,

God cannot fail.

Blood.

A lamb was sacrificed for the redemption of man.

Now, the blood covers a multitude of sin.

STILL

All these wonderful side dishes,

Not to mention the main course of:

God, the Father, which is the head of my life,

Christ the son, who died in my stead.

And the Power of the Holy Ghost,

Which is a heavenly taste.

All this and more, yet my desires were not fulfilled.

When I looked over yonder, and saw another table.

My curiosities did arouse, leaving my taste buds to wonder.

Dinner time at the other table, and there is not enough!

No love.

For love has turned to hate.

Now, hate has turn my heart of flesh to stone.

No charity.

For charity has become stingy

And me, myself, and I have horded in selfishness.

No understanding.

For understanding has turned his back,

And has become unmerciful and uncaring.

No blood.

The blood of the lamb was not identified,

Therefore death and destruction rung out.

No God.

And glory did not shine,

So darkness dwelled therein.

Christ,

The Son of God stood not at all,

For his feet treads not in mulk and miry.

But thank God for the gift of the Holy Ghost,

Because he lived in me,

Just to guide me out.

He returned me to a seat at my Father's table.

Where I can be nurtured on milk and honey.

I can grow to endure the meat and veggies,

So I can grow in spiritual grace.

Here is where I sit,

At the table of righteousness.

With all these delicious dishes,

Soaring to my delight!

God the Father,

Christ the son,

And the Power of the Holy Ghost,

Has fulfilled my wondering appetite!

Unto Thee

Here I stand in all my emptiness, looking to be fulfilled.

Filled with your comforting peace, where no turmoil can exist.

Overrun my life with joy that I may greet each day happily.

Increase the diminishes in my life of faith, as I walk with thee.

Unto thee I cry out for my deliverance,

And I know my pleads shall be heard.

Hear, me oh Lord, my God, when on bended knees I pray,

You are my only assurance in my hour of need.

Restore my soul, for thou are the Son of God,

And I shall be redeemed.

Without you, I am nothing,

Nor shall I ever expect to be.

In appraisal, I am a filthy rag,

And in that light here I stand.

Looking unto thee for an everlasting renewing,

That my regeneration shall surpass time's own infinity.

STILL

I present myself as a living sacrifice,

To be taught of your tender loving mercies,

Teach me humbleness, that I be not haughty in pride.

Unto thee I come in search of perfection,

A perfection whose existence is only by you.

Let all my fallibilities cease, and become infallibilities.

Let not my struggling be in vain,

But let the shouts of victory roar.

When I come to thee as a child, trusting in thy every word.

Looking for leadership, guidance, and understanding,

With all my hopes and dreams for tomorrow.

But as for today, take me as I am, as I come unto thee.

Until Death Do Us Part

All mine,

All yours,

Will become one

As we join hand in hand.

Looking not to the right,

Nor to the left,

But up ahead,

To see what could be ours,

If only we had you.

There will be trails and tribulations.

We must grow to love, to trust, and to respect.

For one another, we must strive to proclaim destiny.

Yours.

Mine.

Will someday be as one.

To be of comfort through life's journey.

For every man there is that certain woman,

That fills his every need.

In proof, I am that woman,

Whose love cannot be surpassed.

Matched by none other,

For there is not another created of my caliber.

And it is that calibration,

Which binds us in perfect harmony.

But, we must keep fast to faith,

For in faith we have hope,

And in our hopes, we have Christ,

To bring us through until death do us part.

Build In Me

Lord, build in me the patience of Job,

That I may see your face.

Enable me to withstand the burdens,

With your wonderfulness.

And when I have done my best,

Let me come out as pure gold.

Build in me that substance of faith,

Which started out as a mustard seed.

Let it flourish that I may gather strength,

In times of battle to hold my peace

And let the Lord fight for me.

In me build the character of perfection

That my mirror image shall be of thee.

Keep me humble, by your hand, am I prosperous.

Let me always bless the Name of the Lord.

For he is blessed.

Build in me fear of the Lord.

To fear thee is to love thee.

Keep me humble, by your hand, am I prosperous

Let me always bless the name of the Lord.

For he is blessed.

Build in me fear of the Lord.

To fear thee is to love thee

Give me the ability to caress that fear,

That I may serve thee more purely.

Oh Lord, when I look heaven's way,

I see your marvelous works,

I awe to imagine the power of your wondrous hands.

All you have created is perfect.

I thank you for being my God.

In every facet of my life let me know,

That you are that rock of salvation,

I am building on.

In You

There are times in life,

When all my struggling seems in vain.

There are times when I feel I cannot go on.

Neither knowing which way my feet shall carry me,

Always seeking, but finding bitter disappointment,

Leaving my heart all beaten and bruised.

Even tearing apart the very essence of my soul.

And in all my wondering ways I know I have you.

In you I find the reasons to greet every morning,

And lift my head toward heaven's way to say thanks.

I have found the humbleness to bow on bended knees,

To say thank You Lord, for just another day.

In you I have peace of mind,

For you are my burden bearer.

And close to you, I will be safe and warm.

In you, I have found the strength to carry on.

STILL

All my life you stood at the door knocking,

Waiting to be invited to share my abode.

I opened that door one day, and I am so glad I did,

Because in you Jesus, I have found a friend.

Behind every gray cloud of darkness,

I can see the light of day.

I feel the peace your love bestows,

To stand fast boldly, and proclaim my destiny.

In you I find the beauty in everything.

Your blood covers a multitude.

For your namesake, does love work wonders,

To provide me with serenity.

In you, I find no other who can compare,

To your gentleness which be stills my soul.

Give me the courage to face life,

As I live on a higher plain.

In you, I have learned to believe in possibilities,

When fallibilities creep in to deter my faith.

In faith do I walk closer, as my soul cries out,

"Yea Lord, I believe in you!"

There IS A Continuation

All my life I have heard,

You live and you die.

And as long as you live,

You are going to owe somebody.

But since I have been born again,

Everything has been rearranged.

My eyes have been opened.

Death holds no bars!

Transgressions are surpassed,

Throughout all infinity,

Iniquities are forgotten,

By the bruise upon his knee.

Yes, I can see there is a continuation,

Through his death, life everlasting.

I can shout alleluia!

Thank God my soul has been set free.

I Am Blessed

I am human, created in the image of God.

Yet, man sees nothing but my status symbol.

Never will he see the real beauty found in me.

I am woman, created to stand by the side of man.

To be his traveling companion,

Therefore, God has made woman to be a man's wife.

God created man in his image,

To feel the beauty wrought by his hand.

Created man, to serve him with purity.

To trust his every word to fulfill his promises,

With each individual living on one accord,

More than willing to be a child of the Lord.

Even though God's plan was intervened upon,

I am truly blessed, because of a redemptive plan.

No more sickness, death, or doubts,

God has sent his only son.

STILL

With an act of unselfish love, he died for me.

That I may live my life worry free,

And for all that I am, I am truly blessed.

TONY HARRIS

With God's Own Love

With God's own love,

Was I nurtured from above.

With his own hand,

Was I delivered into the land.

To live life carefree,

And let all worries pass before me.

Looking for guidance and leadership through every adventure.

I know God will be there; that's for sure.

When all has stood aside and gone as far as they could.

His steadfastness, stood still where I would,

Leading me with strength and sheer determination.

Even when I cannot find my way,

He shows me tender loving mercies from day to day.

And it was God's own love that carried me,

Away from a land of desolation.

He brought me to a place of grace,

Where all is as one nation.

STILL

As I live my life, I shall dare to do my best.

When persecution strives to return my soul to the rest,

I shall hold my head up high toward the stars,

And look as far as I can and know in my heart he cares.

Yes, for God's own love, does my heart yearns.

When I am weak, he is strong.

By God's own love do I thrive,

That let's me know, I will survive.

Come

Lord, come into my life and make me whole.

Fill me with the desire to return.

Use my life to brighten the darkest day,

And let your light shine through me.

Come and let the world see,

The new being I could be.

Let me start afresh each moment,

That I may be able to obtain understanding.

Let me be not vain, for there is nothing I have.

Come in, the door is open, supp with me.

Tell me of all your wondrous works to come.

Show me the richness of thy love.

Teach me from my childhood unto my old age.

That my soul may reach perfection.

Come Lord, hold my hand,

Throughout this long lonely journey.

And if I should faint along the way,

Let it be your hands that carry me.

It is so easy to turn away, and so hard to return.

Finding the straight and narrow is difficult.

I know the way is rough, and I know the way is hard.

Help me Lord, here I come.

Draw Me

Sometimes I look in the mirror, and don't like what I see.

My beauty has been tarnished, look what the world had done.

My eyes look upon the perversions of death,

And see them as the joys of life.

My ears, how they listen,

To slanderous jest, and backbiting alibis.

My mouth smirks in mockery, and laughter.

My body yearns for sin,

And fulfills all the pleasures thereof.

My hands are in idleness, and have no good works,

Easily becomes the devil's workshop.

My feet run the wide open rages, with no direction to turn or go.

Yes, I look in the mirror, and don't like at all what I see.

There is no direction, confusion is all about.

My heart is heavy laden, and the burdens I cannot bare.

The world has trampled me.

In those moments of solitude, reflections of my life,

STILL

I am thankful Jesus is there,

Where I can whisper and say, Lord draw me.

Draw my eyes to look at the perversions of sin,

And in them detest.

Draw my ears away from slanderous jest, and backbiting alibis.

Draw my mouth closed so they speak not from me.

Draw my body into a holy temple, a living sacrifice.

Draw my hands into creativity, and fill their idleness.

Draw my feet nearer to thee, and be a light unto my path.

Uplift my soul, and rejuvenate my spirit.

My heart cries out in joy!

"I don't care how the wild wind rage,

As long as Jesus is drawing me."

Who Can Question?

The stars shine to give the night light.

The sun rises early in the morning to greet the new day.

The east wind blows to and fro, rustling through the trees.

The rain falls from heaven to replenish the earth.

The ocean roars from seashore to seashore.

Oh how magnificent the earth has been made.

Who can question the earth turning to generate gravity?

Who can question the mysteries that have remained so?

Who can question the author's completion of verse and prose?

Is it not the creator who is greater than his creation?

Yet the creation stands boldly in beauty for all to see.

Death does reign and birth does come.

Such as a man live, so shall it return.

Arise, the dawning of a new day has come.

The night has passed.

How can anyone question the alpha and the omega?

How can anyone question the presence of the Almighty?

His purpose?

His life?

And His death?

When all the wonders of science have been left dumbfounded.

Is He not the Creator?

The Author?

And the Finisher of fate,

To give everlasting life to those intent to please?

Who can question the love, that precedes his soul?

Who can question his reasons for living and giving?

Who can question Jesus' most powerful hand?

Who?

Nobody can!

As A Child

Life is full of wonders.

All people contemplate all facets of life.

Everyone must believe in something,

Dream their dreams and fulfill their goals.

As a child I have learned to respect them

I have learned to grow in grace.

To trust and believe with intensity my Father's every word.

A learned trust is a bought trust,

And once learned, it is paid in full.

It is that trust I must follow,

That my dreams may be accomplished.

As a child, I must be taught simple honesty.

As a child of the King, I suffer not for anything.

I can ask for and receive all that is good for me.

Knowing my Father has my best interest at heart,

I look forward to seeing what my Father has for me.

STILL

With heaven as His throne and earth as His footstool,

What is contained therein that I cannot receive?

He looks out for His child as a Father should.

In that security I have His word to stand upon.

His word justifies, and His blood covers me.

He sees me when the wild wind rage, and calms the storm.

That I may continue to grow in grace, as a child.

Bring Out

Everyone has talent.

A special gift that sets them aside from all the rest.

According to faith,

When nurtured, grows.

As a symbol, a trademark, a signature,

To withstand the test of time.

Throughout all infinity it is that signature,

That seals one's fate.

The Author is known by His works,

And His works are known by Him.

It is I who shall bring out.

Out of the heart and soul shall I bring them.

That we may reach the concept of this universe's most single factor.

I shall bring out all that is within you to see.

To understand, to love, to cherish the beauty that thrives.

STILL

As the Author, I will add and take away.

I will bring out the purity of love sought after.

An ultimate love, never to fade away.

Never will love be denied.

It is my symbol that seals your fate.

I stand before you to caress your soul,

And fill your heart with light.

I am the light of the world,

And there's no darkness within.

In you I shall bring out all darkness.

I will add.

I will subtract,

For it is by my hand that you are.

He Talks To Me

He is the still small voice I continue hearing,

In moments of despair, He comes and comforts me.

He tells me of the wonderfuls my soul long to hear.

Gladness comes into my heart when He talks to me.

He is the bright and shining light I see,

As I travel through this darken tunnel of life.

Where I shall stand before His throne.

He is justifying my soul before the Most High.

And as I listen, it soothes my heart to know He speaks for me.

He is the happiness that I feel so early in the morning.

For in Him I know that I am safe from harm.

And when the day has reached its darkest end,

I know I am in Jesus' arms.

As I travel this barren land,

I shall go on, because He talks to me.

STILL

He tells me of His purpose, His living and His giving.

He shows me the treasures of life to seek after.

To follow the dreams I dream as He walks with me.

He teaches me how to live life in all simplicity.

That when complexities arise,

I can go through with joy.

Because He carries my burdens and lightens my heavy load.

It is so great to know that He is my friend,

On this lonely road I travel.

As I walk this journey, striving for all that is right.

I need Him to tell me the way to go.

For His namesake does He cultivate my heart and soul,

To seek after perfection.

For one day I will enter my Father's house,

Without spot or blemish,

Singing the victory, the glory, and the praise,

Thanking Jesus always for talking to me.

I Am Learning

When there is no place to go,

When there is no food to eat,

Or nowhere to lay my head,

I can depend on the Lord.

He is there when I call His name.

He will comfort me when I am distressed.

Jesus loves me for me, and takes me as I am,

Makes me glad to know, He is my savior and friend.

He cares for me as I learn to love Him.

I put my all and all in His hands.

For without Him, I am nothing,

Nor shall I ever expect to be.

I am learning to strive for all that is right.

Though I am weak, you are strong.

You have the power of heaven and earth,

STILL

There is nothing within I can't obtain.

I am learning to trust my life to you,

For my all and all, will I trust upon the Lord.

On The Wings Of Love

I am sailing high above the stratosphere,

And beyond the Milky Way.

I am on the wings of love,

Being carried far away.

In the darkest hour,

I see the light of day.

In my troubles and woes,

I know his love carries me.

I am his.

He is mine.

We are one to proceed through life's journey.

Should I stumble and fall along the way,

His comforting arms will caress me.

Should a tear fall from my eye,

His hand will wipe away the stain.

When I am broken hearted and broken spirited,

Up he lifts my soul on the wings of love.

I am his.

He is mine.

We have that binding love built on a firm foundation,

Of trust, faith, and understanding.

In my flight, I trust in my Lord.

In Him I believe everything is a reality.

And it is that understanding of faith,

Which allows me to forever cling to the wings of love.

Because Of You

Because of you, I am all that I am.

I am grateful for the tender mercies,

You have shown.

Your blood makes me strong.

Because you have instilled in me,

The ability to love and be loved.

You have given me the strength,

To carry on.

Because of you, I can obtain anything.

I can fulfill my dreams, and obtain my goals.

That the world may see,

My Father's love radiates in me.

I am weak, for I am human,

And there is none greater than I.

But you look beyond all my iniquities,

And supply my necessities.

For a child of the King.

Suffers not need of anything.

And it is because of you,

I shall have, all I should have.

Marching On

I cannot look back wondering,

What could I have done to make things better?

Nor, can I stop the road I am traveling.

I must keep marching on.

I keep marching on through His goodness and grace.

He protects me, in this soul drenching fight.

My Lord has prepared a place of rest,

That I may lay my burdens, as I march on.

I keep marching on.

So the good I do, the world may praise my God.

I keep marching on in the service of the Lord.

Never doubting the road I must travel to victory.

Never will I stand alone struggling to survive.

It is for life everlasting that I must fight.

For I keep marching on with the Christ,

Into His Kingdom called eternity.

Only For A Moment

My life span is only a moment,

Whereby I am born, and whereby I must die.

And deter not in faith.

Though the way is hard, this battle must be fought.

Today, choose ye your choice, and stand by your faith.

Walk with your hand held tightly to mine.

As you live, so shall you die.

With my eyes do I see, the Lord cares for me.

I am His and He is mime.

He teaches me to cherish His power.

If only for a moment, I shall call upon His name.

His peace is a place to rest.

Moments when I re-evaluate me,

I find nothing of meaning or value.

In Him I find answers to all the reasons why.

He has been inside of me measuring out His faith.

God has been a real and true God to me.

He accepts me for what I am,

And loves me just the same.

He takes me by and by to a higher plain.

Never has not a need been met.

If I suffered along the way,

It was only for a moment.

And it is that monumental moment,

In which I choose Christ the Lord!

The Fire Burns!

It's Hot!

It's Hot!

The fire really burns!

Because it is Jesus turn!

It yearns and yearns,

For all the knowledge it can learn.

The fire burns and burns,

From way down deep inside.

And even if I wanted,

It will not be denied!

For there is no flickering flame,

That will be taken in stride.

Once seen,

You will run and shout!

Grab another by the hand to see what's about!

It's hot!

It's hot!

The fire really burns!

It's hot!

It's hot!

Come and see what Jesus got!

For You

I see the footprints in the sand,

Running to save my life.

My sorrows are great and my fears are many.

My burdens are heavy and my strength is so weak.

I am dying, I have no reason to live.

My walk was slowed when I waited and wanted.

A love that was never really meant to be.

Now love has left me to die.

But I see my true love running to save me.

Forgive my transgressions, and protect me from my fears.

To you, I pray, love me all the worst of my days,

That I may look up and see your shining face.

Should I ever need reassurance of my true love.

Show me, I was always meant for you.

All Things Are New

New wine has been put in a new bottle,

To expand the depth and height.

All things of old has been put aside,

They are no longer of use.

I have seen the curtain of memory,

A life in which I can never return.

I must accept that is true.

And to accept that is a hard matter to do.

In me there is imperfection.

You touch me and only see the perfection.

You guide the perfect man into the truths of life.

Whether I live or whether I die,

Lord always work with that perfect man,

That my old self may become a new self.

STILL

Able me to thank you for the manna from heaven.

Let my old self look at the new self and smile.

I have come a long way accepting what is true.

Though I can never return yesterday for today,

Nor tomorrow to this moment.

I can look forward with gladness,

That all things are made new.

Life Goes On

The sun will rise bright.

And will set as the day ends.

Each day brings forth trials and tribulations.

You can deal with them?

Run from them?

Hide from them?

Run!

Run!

Run!

Where can you hide?

When life goes on, why even try?

Stand and stay with the goals you have inside.

Live your life one day at a time.

Deal with the present, do not dwell on the past.

Let the future greet you tomorrow.

Tomorrow is the dawning of a brand new day.

Live for now, prepare for later,

Let not wondering thoughts destroy you.

Life is to be lived, loved, and learned.

Because life does go on, so shall you.

Keep Me

No matter what I am to accomplish,

Let me always look to thee.

Let me gather strength from your endured ability.

Enable your love to keep me going on.

Where would I be without you?

Keep me humble in my time of victory.

Because you have brought me out.

Let me be able to call upon your name.

When I can see no hope.

There is power in the name of Jesus!

And it is that power which fills my hopes.

Through Your Eyes

There are things I cannot see,

Nor can I began to comprehend.

Neither can I understand starving when there is plenty.

Am I so blind I cannot see,

The troubles and woes of strife?

What a shame not to see,

The turmoils this land possess.

With your eyes let me behold these injustices,

Which are lashed out at the children of the world.

Let me look upon the pains and sufferings of today.

That reflections of my blessings shall be greatly received.

With your eyes, let me see the things I cannot see.

With your mind, let me grasp the thoughtfulness of you ways.

That I may taste the sweetness of victory.

For I will have learned the most valued lessons,

To share what God has given.

Because there are those who have not.

Let me be not judgmental or critical of things I know not.

But enable me to see memories of the past,

That I may enjoy the future through your eyes.

Reflecting

When I knew not your name to call,

There you stood watching over me.

Making sure I rise early in the morning,

After protecting me during the night.

I sit here reflecting upon my life,

When mama turned against me,

Lord in my life you came.

When papa asked me to leave his abode,

Lord you came again.

Even when my best friend turned against me,

Lord there you stood showing me,

That you are all I need!

Your brought me through the raging storms in my life.

You let me see the light of day.

In myself, when there is no confidence,

You instill in me faith and love.

I find myself reflecting of things old and new,

And in all of my reflections, I see you.

I Took One Step

I took one step and here I came,

Where there are fears and doubts.

Although it seems strange, I feel at home.

A home I have not had since before I went astray.

I learned too much too fast.

Never had I the chance, to know the real me.

Or the opportunity to know life in innocence

Always having to do or die, and damn the what.

Again, I found myself surviving defeat.

Satan greets me with the glamour of death.

Hell teases and taunts me,

Forever clinging on to me.

I took one step away,

From the hustle and bustle of life's grandeur.

To where life is lived in simplicity.

Truth and honestly abides within.

Now I have a chance to grow in grace,

To live my life in peace and harmony

I am glad I took one step away from the world,

Because today is the first day of my life.

A Taste of Heaven

Amazing grace, how sweet it sounds,

Happiness from on high delights my soul.

Shrills from inside burst openly!

How glad I am for a taste of heaven!

Just enough to make me go on.

Forever praying my love will grow stronger.

I will outrun my slow pace to the quickest!

Oh a little taste of heaven does my soul glad!

I watch, listen, and learn of your undying love,

Sent to me from a place high above.

Makes my tears of sadness, those of joy.

How delicious is the taste of heaven!

When all my thoughts are scattered,

Jesus gives me peace of mind.

He removes all my feelings of loneliness,

And adds just a warming touch,

To taste a bit of heaven!

Dreams

Dreams are extensions of the future.

They are pathways to obtainable goals.

Therefore, dream on into eternity

It is today that dreams are fulfilled.

What is life without dreaming?

No man can, because dreaming is the soul of God.

In my dreams, I live life exceedingly.

They give me direction in my everyday life.

And when I try to reflect upon them,

I live through Christ.

There is nothing I cannot accomplish without dreaming,

Dreams are a continuation of forever.

To forever the dreamer dreams of Christ,

And in Him are all my dreams fulfilled.

I Have Lived My Dream

Lord, you know so much about me.

Yes, you know it all.

I have been through so much,

I have cried out for help.

And where is my help, except it be by thee?

I have given my all and all!

Oh Lord, when all is dark before my eyes,

Whose name can I call unless it be thine?

I have lived with hope and determination.

Tomorrow is a brand new day,

And this day has gone forever.

And I shall awake tomorrow morning,

With all my problems before me,

But, I have lived a dream beautiful in everyway.

I have lived my dream through.

STILL

And if I had it to do over again, I would.

Because I have learned the courage it takes to make it!

I have learned the glory,

That surpasses all my struggling.

I shall never forget,

The one who has been there for me.

Thanking you for all that has been said and done.

As I live my dream into reality.

This IS Mine

I have tried many things.

Sometimes, I've failed.

Sometimes, I've succeeded.

I have searched for that one point in life,

That makes it worth living.

At every twist and turn,

Walls were built before me.

No matter what, I keep on trying!

Knowing there is got to be a better way.

And though there are not many things I can claim,

I can say, "Yes Lord this is mine".

I have a choice.

And in that choice, I choose the Christ.

He is mine.

Through all my tribulations, and trails

My heart is glad to know that you are there.

STILL

You listen to me.

You cry with me.

You give me strength to go on!

You laugh with me,

Knowing the true victory is mine.

In that light,

I claim all that is in heaven,

And all that is on earth,

As mine.

Calling On Jesus

Lord, you know the problems that face me.

My entire life is on the line.

There is nothing more important,

Than life's hopes and dreams.

The endless chores of working them out,

Through those dreams I found your glory.

I have found a closer walk with you.

For the past year, I have sought a career.

I have studied, and I have pressed.

I have given my all and all.

I have stumbled and I have fallen.

I have cried out, "Lord help me,"

surely thou are the rock in a weary land!

Today is like forever Lord,

Because of all the problems confronting me

I cannot succumb to them, though.

STILL

I just cannot let Satan win

For a new zeal has awakened in me.

Tomorrow is another day. To hell with the past!

Long live Christ as my future.

You Fixed It For Me

Whew Lord!

You did it for me!

I shouted out your praise!

Joy has filled my soul!

You fixed my problems.

You placed a roof over my head,

When I was being kicked out the door.

You supplied the strength it took,

To pass the test of my life.

Oh Lord, you made a way,

When I saw no way.

Yes, you fixed everything.

Though I am not worthy, you justified me.

And you have given me new mountains to climb.

You fixed my feet on higher grounds.

Thank you.

STILL

Your praise shall never leave me.

Without you Father, I am dead.

But with you, I can accomplish anything.

Because I know you'll be there to fix it for me.

Outside The Storm IS Raging

The world outside is raging.

Raging in madness trying to pull me in,

Trying to deter my faith.

No!

I will not go running to here and there,

Trying to fight this raging madness,

But I shall stay here, and hide my cleft in thee.

Outside, the storm is raging.

But, I have found peace in all this confusion.

I have learned to trust you for my all and all.

For you have proven yourself strong.

Outside, the storm is raging.

Full force ahead.

Snatching and gnawing at my very existence.

Yet, I shall not die,

This terrible storm shall be the triumph of the Lord's!

STILL

He takes me by and by,

And shelter me from the wiles of the storm.

In peace he shelters me because,

Outside, the storm is raging on.

Hinder Me, But Don't Stop Me!

Go ahead and hinder me,

With your evilness.

Smile in my face,

Then stab me in my back.

Go ahead and try me,

But don't stop me.

Hinder, and hold up all good blessings,

You have that right.

To prevent my God from my sight.

Do as you must, but don't stop me.

It's even okay

If you close the door in my face.

Hinder me, if you can.

If it gives you joy, go ahead.

If it gives you peace of mind,

Hinder me, but you will never stop me!

It Doesn't Really Matter

Satan, you have tried this and that,

And, still you try to bruise my head.

Then you stab me in my back.

But that is all right.

It doesn't really, matter what you do.

I will sit here, and wait upon the Lord.

I will look at you.

I will see you for who and what you are.

I will laugh at you.

I have God's sheltering arms all about.

So it doesn't really matter,

How much you make the strong wind rage,

Or how rough you make the rolling seas.

Even in your boldness you forget!

My Lord makes peace be still.

And though you may laugh outwardly,

Inwardly, you are boiling mad.

For Christ is the head of my life,

And Him only do I fear.

Do you see, nothing you do matters to me,

Not one iota at all.

Your stupidness is your own pity.

In fact you are the very one,

Who should ask forgiveness,

Because of your selfishness,

The whole world is in remorse.

I am A Child God

Who are you?

What do you stand for?

Do not let the world take your joy!

I am a child of God.

Sometimes I am even considered a nobody.

But, I will have peace and joy.

From this day forth,

They will despise the sight of me.

They will feel shame.

They will be confounded.

With humility will I greet them.

For as long as there is another day,

There is a better day.

I will thank the Lord for all his blessings.

I will praise him all day long,

With words,

With deeds,

With my all and all,

Because I am a child of God.

The Way

Walking in the way,

Gets sweeter and sweeter by day.

The way of thankfulness!

The way of praise!

For the victory has already been won!

Lord you know I am sick,

And here you are with me.

Comforting me with words,

That I will praise your name.

Lord, You keep comforting me through it all.

You keep showing me the way I must follow.

"For the way is easy, you can leave all your troubles there."

Yes Lord walking in the way,

Gets sweeter and sweeter.

I can smile in all my fears and doubts,

Thanking you and worshipping you,

In my own special way.

Lord I was about to be homeless,

But you knew that too.

All else has failed to come to my need.

None, expect thee oh Lord has fulfilled.

At rest I am, with somewhere to lay my head.

"Yes, walking in the way will make everything all right."

By and by, my Lord,

The way gets sweeter and sweeter.

Everyday, let the praises of the most High

Fill my every existence,

That I may cherish all sought after.

Yes, walking in the way of thankfulness and praise,

Gets sweeter and sweeter day by day.

For thou are the Lord of my life.

You keep proving the way I should go.

Thank you Lord, for I shall follow the way with you.

STILL

When Times Draw Nigh

Oh Lord,

Is it always darkest before the dawn?

Then if so, it looks pretty bad,

This dark dawn approaching.

Yes Lord, it is a battle I must face,

Times are drawing nigh.

Oh Lord, when I must go down in the valley,

Weakened in my endurance,

Let the storm pass over,

That I should see the glory of morn.

Lord,

Let me hide my cleft in thee, as you intercede,

That my endurance may be strengthen,

Where am I without you?

Where is my strength if not found in thee?

Where would I go to seek shelter from the storm?

If not to your abode.

And now that the darkest before dawn has risen,

Be there oh Lord, at the light of day.

When times draw nigh, give me serenity within,

To know that you are drawing me nigh to thee.

The Curtains of Memories

Roll back the curtains.

Bring back the memories of old.

To times which has taught me,

To trust upon the Lord.

In times of tribulation,

I have cried out to the Lord.

And He answered my call.

There is my warrior fighting my battle!

Then He delivers me into the valley,

On His wings of love.

I look back at a time,

When I needed direction,

Even reasons to live just one more day.

You came and gave me a purpose,

A reason for living and giving.

You have shown to me my best.

You have shown me at the worst.

You have enabled me to see.

The difference you make in me.

Oh Lord, when I see the new self,

I see your mighty hands sculpturing my soul.

You have taken this muddy lump of clay,

And created me a woman,

That I must suffer all the pains,

Of a time so long ago.

The curtains of memories rolls on.

I see the faith that you have given me.

To believe in my dreams,

And live them through into reality!

Roll back the curtains of memories!

He has transplanted my roots to rich moist soils!

And given me a reason,

STILL

To challenges life's uncertainties,

With the factuality of Christ.

Blame Not

Blame not the child.

He is only the seed that grew.

But blame the rocky soil that inhibited growth,

Leaving the plant to quickly wither away.

Blame not the outcome of fate.

But the incidents and circumstances which led to.

Life unfolds many facets,

And into each facet is that learning tree,

Whereby the seed must be transplanted,

To the rich moist soil.

Blame not the farmer,

Whose wheat grew up with tares.

But blame the evil one.

In his wickedness did he try to destroy good.

While the good farmer laughs ha! ha! to his face.

For he knows the skill and grace of the tiller's hand.

No!

Blame not the child

For his fallibilities,

When no one has not shown him possibilities.

Where dreams are fulfilled and goals are accomplished.

No!

Blame not the child,

Who cannot see Christ.

People Do Not Know

The world is confused.

Everyone running to and fro,

Trying to find answers for life's problems.

No one really seeing the issues,

Between good and evil,

Life and death,

God and satan.

Some feel it is within their power to justify abortion.

To determine the breath of God,

Is such a foolish chore.

Another confusion of satan,

To destroy the image of God,

That being,

Man.

Some believe it is merciful,

Not to suffer when life draws nigh.

They take the easy way to death,

But forget about the eternal being,

An act by which death is good,

But welcomed by whom?

God?

No! God gives life, not death.

In the final end,

The soul suffers eternal damnation.

Satan welcoming eternal torment,

For those who have fallen and died.

Life, death, good and evil,

Are they not counterparts of God and Satan?

These issues, people do not understand,

The war between God and Satan is real!

Each standing up fighting and dying for their beliefs.

The senseless blood spilled upon the soil,

Cries out in agony and defeat,

Father, the people do not know.

Talent

Everyone is given talent,

With which, we must praise the Lord.

My gift, a very special talent indeed.

My hands create wondrous words of wisdom,

And bring it to simple explanation.

God has given me that talent,

To praise Him with words.

People say I am funny though, I see it not.

They encourage me to seek fame and fortune,

Through the gift of laughter.

I am but, a vessel,

To be filled with all manner of goods.

And if those goods be of the Lord's

The I am valuable.

God has endowed me with talent.

Now the time has risen,

STILL

When I must take my measured talent,

Toss it upon the waters,

And watch the return.

I sit, as a candle, upon a far off distant hill,

That all may see my light.

For in my light lives Christ.

And there is no accomplishment I want,

If it does not exist in him.

I shall cast forth my talents.

In all I attempt to do.

Through words, thoughts, actions, and deeds,

That the earth may rejoice in His glory with me.

Whatever

Whatever I want to do, I can.

All it takes is faith.

To see what the eyes cannot see,

And live it through until reality.

Whatever my heart delights can be me.

Through patience and longsuffering.

Nobody said it would be easy,

But through perseverance can I obtain anything.

Whatever the wiles of tomorrow,

I will gather up strength,

To proceed forth,

And proclaim my destiny in whatever!

Facets

To the tree are many branches.

Each branch glorifying the tree.

What is the tree, but the basis of its limbs?

Branching forth the intricate facets beautifying the tree.

The roots are entwined deep within rich moist soil.

That life may endure throughout generations.

Living through the many facets of times' own infinity.

Changing daily in growth,

Knowing that no two days are ever the same.

For today must it stand in luster,

Binding its many facets into the glory of the tree.

I Can Say

Lord, you see the afflictions and attritions.

But that's all right, you see.

Lord you know the uncertainties I face.

But that's all right, you know.

In all things I can say thank you.

Lord, you have shown me so many things,

Facets of life, I have yet to understand.

Circumstances to the cause and effect of outcome.

Lord you have accepted me as I am,

Now I can accept me.

My qualities as well as my inequalities.

Now, I can accept the changes you make in me.

Lord through all times you stand and lead,

The way I am to follow.

You have proven yourself a mighty warrior in deed.

That only a mite as I can say, thank you.

Teach Me Humbleness

Lord teach me humbleness

As we travel the road together.

That I may look to thee.

Let me be not boastful of any accomplishment.

But let the world see my Father.

Let me not claim any good thing I do.

Only by your hand am I able.

Look down upon the earth and consider.

Teaching me humbleness.

Stand before me and protect me.

Keep me from all hurt and harm.

As you entrap my mind with rest,

Lord, teach me humbleness.

I Shall

When I cry out in distress,

Because of the burdens that press.

When I dry my weeping eyes,

I shall wait upon the Lord.

Where is my peace if not found in Him?

Where am I to lay my weary head?

The world works against my soul.

Oh Lord, I shall wait for my strength.

I shall sing praises,

And count my blessings.

I shall keep my eyes Heaven-way,

And await a wondrous work.

Oh Lord, when I bow before thee,

I shall humble myself, for you are great.

I shall bring you all my problems,

Because you are my problem solver.

STILL

Lord you know everything,

Both big and small.

I shall gather myself unto thee,

And let your blood cover me.

When I am hungry, I shall be fed.

When I am homeless, I shall be sheltered.

When I wake to see a new day

I shall see Christ the King!

Watch Out!

He is out there.

Lurking to and fro,

Searching for the child of God,

To catch you unaware.

Watch out as you travel,

From darkness into light.

He is mad!

He is ready to attack,

Because on him you have turned your back.

He is just outside the door,

Marching back and forth,

Trying this and trying that,

Setting up obstacles in your way.

Watch out! Watch out I say!

He is out there,

STILL

On your job, and in your car,

He is out there, whenever you are.

Tell him once. Tell him twice.

The Lord is the head, and you are the tail.

His blood cleanses, and washes white as snow.

Watch out my child, and look at me.

Do not fear at all what you see.

I have always been here, right inside.

Guiding you through the rough and rocky storms.

And giving you my shoulder to lean upon.

Watch out!

He is ready you can bet.

But you just keep believing,

I have not left you yet.

That is why I warn,

Watch out my child, watch out!

TONY HARRIS

With My

With my mind's eye do I see,

A new pilgrimage for me,

With new heights to climb,

And dreams to dream,

Does my Lord prepare for me.

With my hands do I praise him.

With words of simplicity that sound so sweet.

With my feet, shall I follow.

The whims of my every tomorrow.

For today he tests me, wither I shall go.

With my own judgment, do I judge myself,

And find my worth of naught.

If it were my final judgment,

Then for true, I would be lost.

With eagerness, do I daily pray,

To strengthen my walk,

That I should never stray,

And be not lost along the way.

Lord teach me and guide me.

Today is a brand new start.

You have taken away the stones,

And given me a new heart.

I am only an instrument,

To be manipulated by my Lord,

In any way he chooses,

With me myself and I,

Am going all the way with Christ.

There Shall Be Rest

I have been fighting my foe without end.

Yes, the very one who has caused me to sin.

And though this fight is not of flesh and blood.

My God I am so tired, I need rest.

I have fought with the enemy at every corner turned.

Gee, I hope I am winning.

With all the energy I have burned.

I am so tired, Lord I need rest.

My nerves are shattered

My body is bruised.

Lord only you know the stress endured.

What I need so much so is rest.

Sometimes I laugh,

And sometimes I cry.

For soon the battle will be over,

And there shall be rest.

The Smile?

What is the smile?

Is it the greeting upon one's face?

Will the smile show the true inner self?

Or perhaps, the smile may reflect the outer self?

This thing the smile must be searched?

Is the smile real?

Does it show truth and sincerity?

Or is the smile false?

Showing only vengefulness and hate?

Is it something as knives or as honey?

Should the smile be taken at worth?

Yes, this thing the smile, must be searched.

And should be taken for its worth.

The smile is the inner reflected outwardly,

And can be seen for all one's worth!

Even Though

Lord, even though it be,

The wee, wee hours of morn,

I can raise my head Heaven-way

And be thankful for another day.

Even though the nigh is still,

Satan is not.

His alertness in the slumbering hours,

Fills my life with dread.

In my waking hours,

Does my soul delight,

Because I can think of my Lord's goodness,

Through the struggle and the strife.

Yes Lord, I know he watches me.

He hears every word I say,

In the event he may criticize,

My actions and my deeds.

Peace be still my soul,

When I think of Heaven-way

Even though the evil one sits beside me,

Trying me and testing me, to see if I am afraid.

And if the Lord be my strength and my guide?

Whom shall I fear?

My soul gathers strength,

Even in the wee hours of morn,

Because satan is here,

Trying to deter my faith.

With The Quickness

With the flash of an eye,

Let me get up and have my being.

Motivate my slowness to the quickness,

That each movement may be fluent

Moving rhythmically with the quickness.

That no opportunity should be amiss.

Make me outrun myself to my destination.

I will have gathered strength aforetime.

Not to put off for tomorrow,

Lord I pray!

Stop me from procrastinating!

Enable me to see ahead,

Facets of tomorrow,

Let me plant the seed today.

So when tomorrow peaks forth

I will reap my rewards.

Because when tomorrow does come,

It comes with the quickness!

Consume

When my thoughts do wonder astray,

Consume my soul, that I must pray.

For the human part of me,

Does get in the way.

Consume the inner me,

That I may seek your face.

When trouble tries to harm me,

Roaring in its might,

Robe me with courage to stay my fight.

Consume my nothingness,

With praises and things to do.

For idle hands are in that, idle.

Ensnare them and press their business of you.

Captivate my free moments,

With sweet thoughts of you.

That I may grow in grace,

And someday see your face.

Lead me and guide me forever and a day,

As I follow thee along the way.

Consume me when I least expect it,

To be on fire for the Lord.

Sunrise to Glory

The night is filled with all sorts of dread.

Sometimes it is hard to even lift my head,

Or even just to share a smile.

For the darkness abounds mile after mile.

And yet I look forward to see day.

Because when daylight comes,

It brings a brighter joy.

More joyous than I have ever known,

For I can see sunrise to glory.

Right now I may cry,

As the night pass me by,

I will see tomorrow morning,

Bringing in my delight.

For I will have lived through another night.

Just to see sunrise to glory,

Bringing in my joys

With each moment of trail and tribulation,

And all the burdens that press,

Keep me holding onto hope,

In that my hope be forever in Christ,

Because He is my sunrise to glory.

Each and every day as I continually learn.

Let me grasps the understandings,

To the minimum of each part,

And wrap every particle,

Into it's largest mass.

That the light may creep upon darkness,

And color it sunrise to glory.

He Is

He lives!

He can see,

Smell,

Taste,

Move,

And hear.

Whom shall I fear?

He is steadfast.

Forevermore!

Never does he run,

Peep, Or hide.

My God is full of pride.

Who is it that He must fear?

That He must walk away in stride?

He is a warrior.

And though some may say,

He was never born.

Or died,

And never rose.

He is forever,

Yesterday,

Today,

And always,

Alive!

I'm Gonna Live

I'm gonna live my life,

From day to day,

Always looking Heaven-way

I don't care what the world may say,

I'm gonna live from day to day,

Always looking Heaven-way,

I'm gonna live

When I think about

How sweet the sound.

That washed me whiter than snow,

I sing out my praise to you.

Sing of all your mercies, and tender grace,

And await my moment when I shall see your face,

As I live from day to day.

Always looking Heaven-way,

I'm gonna live.

Oh how I love you Jesus,

For you'll never let me stray.

As I walk this journey,

Through thick and thin.

You'll hold me so dearly,

Keep me safe from harm.

Hold fast to me Jesus,

Hold me fast in your arms,

As I live my life from day to day.

I'm gonna live my life

From day to day

Always looking Heaven-way.

I don't care what the world may say

I'm gonna live from day to day

Always looking Heaven-way.

I'm gonna live.

The Rainbow

My granny showed me a rainbow,

As we traveled the long and lonely miles.

She said, don't cry baby,

You don't see any rain today do you?

But look, see, there is a rainbow.

I looked up in the clear blue sunny skies.

 Saw the sparkle of its glory!

The promise I saw was a promise for keeps,

The rainbow granny showed was for me.

The pains are so hard to bear.

But the way is light.

I have no problems.

I have no cares.

My granny showed me a rainbow,

And I know Christ is there.

My Telephone Lover

He calls me.

At first, I thought only to say hello.

And to myself I wondered, surely there must be more.

I can see his radiant smile beaming through the telephone.

When he whispers softly and dear,

I can feel his probing tongue nibbling in my ear.

He calls me everyday.

Never at the same time, mind you.

Because that would take the fun away.

His voice draws fire from my soul.

Almost as if I were a candle flickering,

He cups his hands around my weakened flame.

Never again to flicker the same.

He talks to me,

In smooth rhythmic waves.

He makes me quiver!

STILL

Is he real?

I feel the longingness of my telephone lover.

I can see his soul proclamations of love.

I can taste the bitter-sweet challenges,

His heart sings as he silently cries,

"Come, let me show you the wonders of love

That you may experience the beauty therein"

As I talk to my telephone lover,

I can feel his searching eyes,

Looking and wondering if I am lonely too.

Almost as if he is sitting across from me,

Watching me as I blush under his scrutinizing gaze.

He knows I hate to relinquish his call,

Because of the emptiness that soon follows.

I just finished talking to my telephone lover.

Now, I am burning to be touched.

I am holding myself with my own arms,

Because I'm thinking of you, my dearest.

We

We finally contained the miles,

That separated he and me.

We shared laugher and love,

As we became closer.

We looked expectingly into each other's eyes,

Wanting the tenderness of the other's touch.

He listened as I unveiled mysteries of me.

He watched me as I moved across the floor.

He saw me in my nervousness,

And set my spirit at rest.

He looked into my eyes with such an awesome look

That made me hold my breathe, as my body shook.

I showed him me, myself, and I,

As no one has ever seen.

Or did I?

Maybe it was only a dream.

STILL

I can only hope he felt as I.

That he and me should become we.

We should share all the joys that lovers do.

Yet, maintain our individuality,

As we grow as one.

That we may obtain an everlasting friendship,

Which should be our only foundation,

As he and me become we.

To John Keats

As with Death

The pictures on the Grecian Urn

Are held fast in time

For in these pictures

Beauty has been captivated.

Never to fade away.

They are held motionless,

As the days turn into years

The beauty which lies therein

Shall always be.

Ah, it is better

These scenes are captivated here,

Upon this Grecian Urn.

For if they exist,

In the time frame of reality

STILL

Their beauty would soon pass away

Never again to glisten in beauty.

ABOUT THE AUTHOR

Author Tony Harris is excited about her first published book, "STILL". She thanks God for this collection of inspirational poems. Because God taught her to live in Christ.

Tony is currently employed with Waffle House. She is a member of the International Poetry Society. Her bio is listed in Marquis WHO's WHO. She is a graduate of Iona School of Nursing.

Made in the USA
Columbia, SC
31 January 2018